mother and daughter

friends

of the heart

GIFT BOOKS
from Hallmark

a gift for

_____

with love from

_____

© 2006 Hallmark Licensing, Inc.
www.hallmark.com

Editorial Director: Todd Hafer
Editor: Jeff Morgan
Art Director: Kevin Swanson
Designer: Michelle Nicolier
Production Art: Dan Horton

Printed and bound in China.
ISBN: 1-59530-129-1

First Edition, March 2006
13 12 11 10 9 8 7 6 5 4
BOK4316

always
and forever

There are so many wonderful things
to say about a daughter like you—
but never enough words to
tell you how much *you're loved*.

From the very beginning,

a daughter is a beautiful blend

of *promise* and *possibility*...

...she is hopes and plans,

 what-ifs and whens.

A daughter is the why, the because...

the *always,* and the *forever.*

In a daughter's dreams...

a mother's *hope*.

In a daughter's achievements...

a mother's *pride*.

In a daughter's happiness...

a mother's *joy*.

A daughter is someone you

 laugh and dream with…

and *love* even more

than any hug can say.

Watching her grow
into her own *strong,* sensitive self
is one of the most fulfilling
experiences a mother can know.

A daughter can go
as far as her *dreams*
will take her...

...and wherever she goes,

she is always

close at heart.

A daughter

is thought about often...

always with *love*.

She has a way

of filling days with sunshine…

and filling hearts with *happy memories*.

Like ripples in a pond,
a daughter's life reaches out,
touching others with *happiness.*

A daughter is like a *gift*
wrapped in laughter and dreams...
and trimmed with love.

In her eyes,

the *stars*...

in her smile,

the *sun*.

A daughter grows up quickly,
and just about the time you
begin to miss your "little girl,"
you realize you've found a *friend*.

To have a friend in your daughter

is to know one of the

greatest friendships of all.

Nowhere is it written

that a mother and her daughter

must be friends—

which makes it *even better*

when they are.

Mother and daughter,

friends of *the heart.*

all
we share

With each stage of our lives,

we find new things to *share*

as our bond of family, friendship,

and love remains constant.

And our good times,

those *special moments,*

light up every corner of my world.

Year after year,
together, we learn
a thousand
little lessons of love.

Our close *relationship* with each other

strengthens us and makes

our little victories possible.

There is an understanding,

an intuitiveness,

an easy kind of laughter

that we share because *we're family*...

...and when we laugh so hard

we start crying,

when we cry so long

we end up laughing,

we know how *close* we truly are.

We learn that even
when people irritate
you like crazy,
you can *still love them*.

Some family relationships

are so uplifting and so irritating…

that they can provide

the *greatest joy*

and a lot of aggravation

at the same time.

Love between a
mother and daughter
is complicated,
noisy, tender,
stormy, affectionate,
funny, and *fun.*

There is no problem

that we can't

ignore, discuss, plot against,

make fun of, or

drown in *chocolate sauce.*

To love a daughter,

to show her the way,

and to embarrass her once

in a while in front of her friends…

these are the *duties* of a mom.

And it's also a duty to hope

that every dream

she holds in her heart comes true.

Mother and daughter
are *together*
for the good, the bad,
and the really boring.

A daughter learns
  to *share* ideas, dreams,
    and the makeup
counter gift-with-purchase.

And no one could

ever fill a daughter's shoes.

(After all, she has so many!)

Our blue times

and sunny times—

we hold them

together *with love.*

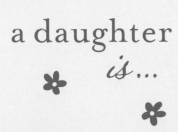

a daughter *is...*

A daughter is the person who
can finish your sentences
and share your *chocolate*.

She is *pleasant chitchat*

and comfortable silence all in one.

I never know when

some happy moment...

will make me think of *you*.

So many favorite stories begin with

"One time, *my daughter* and I...."

✿ Seeing a daughter become a confident woman is one of life's greatest joys.

She carries with her

the strength of her character

and the promise of the *future.*

There is no greater happiness,
no better reason to be *proud*
than watching her
find her place in the world.

In her *achievements,*
a mother's hopes come to life.
She is one of life's brightest lights,
greatest hopes, and purest joys.

She is a source of smiles,

dreams, and *fulfillment*.

There's simply no counting
the *blessings,* the lessons,
the joys that come with a daughter.

The love between mother

and daughter is forever.

It is timeless, beautiful, and *true*.

If you have enjoyed this book.
Hallmark would love
to hear from you.

PLEASE SEND COMMENTS TO
Book Feedback
2501 McGee, Mail Drop 215
Kansas City, MO 64141-6580

OR E-MAIL US AT:
booknotes@hallmark.com